Killer Disasters

THUNDERSTORMS

DOREEN GONZALES

PowerKiDS
press™

New York

Published in 2013 by The Rosen Publishing Group, Inc.
29 East 21st Street, New York, NY 10010

First Edition

Editor: Amelie von Zumbusch
Book Design: Greg Tucker

Photo Credits: Cover swissmacky/Shutterstock.com; p. 4 Mario Villafuerte/Getty Images; p. 5 Ross Ellet/Shutterstock.com; pp. 6–7 Jhaz Photography/Shutterstock.com; p. 8 gary718/Shutterstock.com; pp. 9, 22 kavram/Shutterstock.com; p. 10 Justin Sullivan/Getty Images; p. 11 (right) John Tinning/Photo Researchers/Getty Images; p. 11 (left) Bloomberg/Getty Images; pp. 12–13 Steshkin Yevgenly/Shutterstock.com; p. 14 Mike Theiss/National Geographic/Getty Images; p. 15 (top) HABRDA/Shutterstock.com; p. 15 (bottom) STRDEL/AFP/Getty Images; p. 16 ChinaFotoPress/Getty Images; p. 17 Jerry Sharp/Shutterstock.com; p. 18 Jim Reed/Photo Researchers/Getty Images; p. 19 (main) Tim Boyles/Getty Images; p. 19 (inset) Eric Nguyen/Jim Reed Photography/Photo Researchers/Getty Images; p. 20 SuperStock/Getty Images; p. 21 Chris Johns/National Geographic/Getty Images.

Library of Congress Cataloging-in-Publication Data

Gonzales, Doreen.
Thunderstorms / by Doreen Gonzales. — 1st ed.
    p. cm. — (Killer disasters)
Includes index.
ISBN 978-1-4488-7443-9 (library binding) — ISBN 978-1-4488-7516-0 (pbk.) —
ISBN 978-1-4488-7590-0 (6-pack)
1. Thunderstorms—Juvenile literature. I. Title.
QC968.2.G66 2013
551.55'4—dc23
                          2012004498

Manufactured in the United States of America

CPSIA Compliance Information: Batch #B3S12PK: For Further Information contact Rosen Publishing, New York, New York at 1-800-237-9932

CONTENTS

THUNDER! LIGHTNING!

Rain is pouring down, and the hairs on your arms are standing up. Suddenly **lightning** shoots from the sky, and a loud crack cuts through the air. A thunderstorm has hit! A thunderstorm is a rainstorm with thunder and lightning. Lightning is a flash of electricity. Thunder is the noise that lightning makes when it flashes.

On April 8, 2002, a severe thunderstorm caused tornadoes in Louisiana, Texas, and Arkansas. One of the tornadoes knocked down this tree in Plain Dealing, Louisiana.

Thunderstorms can be dangerous. As the saying goes, "When thunder roars, go indoors!"

Most thunderstorms last about 30 minutes. Severe thunderstorms, however, last much longer. A severe thunderstorm is one that brings **hail**, strong winds, or **tornadoes**. A severe thunderstorm can damage buildings and uproot plants as large as trees. It can even hurt people.

THE CLOUDS ABOVE

Thunderstorms form when there is a lot of warm moisture, or **vapor**, in the air. The vapor rises and cools, forming puffy clouds called **cumulus clouds**.

With enough moisture, cumulus clouds get bigger and their tops grow into tall towers. At this point, they are known as **cumulonimbus clouds**. The air inside them moves upward, forming an **updraft**. At the same time, vapor inside the clouds turns into raindrops. As they fall, they create downward winds called **downdrafts**.

Sometimes the cloud tops spread out to form anvil clouds. These are the kinds of clouds that can turn into a severe thunderstorm.

This cumulonimbus cloud is an anvil cloud. The tops of such clouds are sometimes called thunderheads.

WHERE IN THE WORLD?

Thunderstorms can happen almost anywhere. Some of the strongest thunderstorms happen in Argentina, Australia, Pakistan, and Bangladesh. Thunderstorms are common in the tropics. This is the area around the equator where the air is wet and warm.

This thunderstorm is in Miami, Florida. Central Florida has the most thunderstorms, but they are also quite common along the coasts.

This thunderstorm is sweeping across a field in Montana.

In the United States, thunderstorms happen in every state. Florida has the most thunderstorms. Thunderstorms are least common on the West Coast and in Alaska and Hawaii. Severe thunderstorms are most common in the plains between southern Minnesota and Texas.

Thunderstorms can form in any season. However, they are most common in the spring and summer. They usually happen in the afternoon and evening.

ELECTRIC SKIES

Lightning forms when an **electric charge** builds up in storm clouds. Negatively charged **particles** build up at the bottom of the cloud. They are attracted to positively charged particles in the ground below. The particles stream toward each other, creating a flash of lightning.

Lightning can start fires when it hits buildings or trees. Sometimes lightning strikes people, hurting them badly or even killing them.

Left: Since lightning hits whatever is closest, it tends to strike the highest point. *Right*: The metal rod on this chimney is a lightning rod. If lightning hits, it is drawn to the rod. Its charge travels down the rod into the ground.

The heat from lightning explodes the air around it, making thunder. You see lightning the moment it happens. Sound travels more slowly than light, though. It takes about 5 seconds for sound to travel 1 mile (2 km). You can use the time gap between lightning and thunder to figure out how far away lightning is.

Thunderstorm Facts

Number of thunderstorms each year
in the United States: About 100,000

Average width of a thunderstorm: 15 miles (24 km)

Wind speed at which a thunderstorm
is considered severe: 58 miles per hour (93 km/h)

Average number of Americans killed
by lightning each year: 58

Average number of Americans hurt
by lightning each year: 300

Temperature of the air near
a lightning strike: 50,000° F (27,760° C)

Number of times lightning strikes
in the United States each year: **25 million**

Width of the largest hail: **8 inches (20 cm)**

Heaviest hail: **1.9 pounds (862 g)**

Deadliest hailstorm: **246 people died on April 30, 1888, in India**

ICE FROM THE SKY

Severe thunderstorms sometimes bring hail. Hail forms when an updraft pulls a raindrop high into the clouds, where cold temperatures freeze it. The frozen drop then falls. As it falls, it gets coated with more moisture. Another updraft may carry the drop back up and freeze the new coat of moisture. This can happen several times until the drop is heavy enough to fall to the ground.

Hail from a thunderstorm cracked this car's windshield.

Above: Pieces of hail are sometimes known as hailstones.
Right: This building was destroyed by hail during a 2008 thunderstorm in Guwahati, India.

Hail can grow quite large. Large or small, it can cause a lot of damage. It can destroy plants, dent cars, and tear up roofs. Hail can also hurt people, and large hail has killed people.

WATER IN A FLASH!

Some thunderstorms bring heavy rains that cause flooding. Flooding happens when water flows onto land that is usually dry. Floods can uproot trees, destroy buildings, and carry away cars.

These people got caught in a flood after a big thunderstorm hit Beijing, China, in 2011.

16

People should never drive into floodwaters. The waters are often deeper and more dangerous than they look.

Thunderstorms may cause flash floods. These are floods that happen suddenly. Flash floods most often occur in low areas or in spots where rain flows into narrow places. Flash floods are dangerous because they happen so quickly that people do not have time to get out of their way. About half of the people who die in flash floods are killed when the cars they are driving are swept downstream.

SPINNING WINDS

A tornado is a column of spinning wind. Most tornadoes form in large thunderstorms called supercells. Supercells have strong updrafts that cause vertical columns of spinning wind inside thunderclouds. Tornadoes form when these spinning winds drop from the clouds and touch the ground.

Supercells are sometimes known as rotating thunderstorms. This is because they rotate, or turn.

In 2007, thunderstorms caused a tornado that tore through Lady Lake, Florida, destroying buildings and killing several people. *Inset*: This thunderstorm caused a tornado, hail, and a rainbow!

One thunderstorm can cause many tornadoes. These can happen at the same time or on and off as a storm moves along.

Tornadoes can be 1 mile (2 km) wide and spin at speeds of more than 300 miles per hour (483 km/h). They can blow over buildings, rip trees from the ground, and kill people and animals.

LEARNING ABOUT THUNDERSTORMS

Scientists use **radar** and **satellites** to track thunderstorms. The National Weather Service uses this information to send out warnings to the people in a storm's path. After a thunderstorm, scientists use the information gathered by radar and satellites to study how the storm grew and moved.

Benjamin Franklin showed that lightning was electricity by flying a kite with a key tied to it in a thunderstorm. Unlike some stories say, he did not hold the kite's string, as that is dangerous.

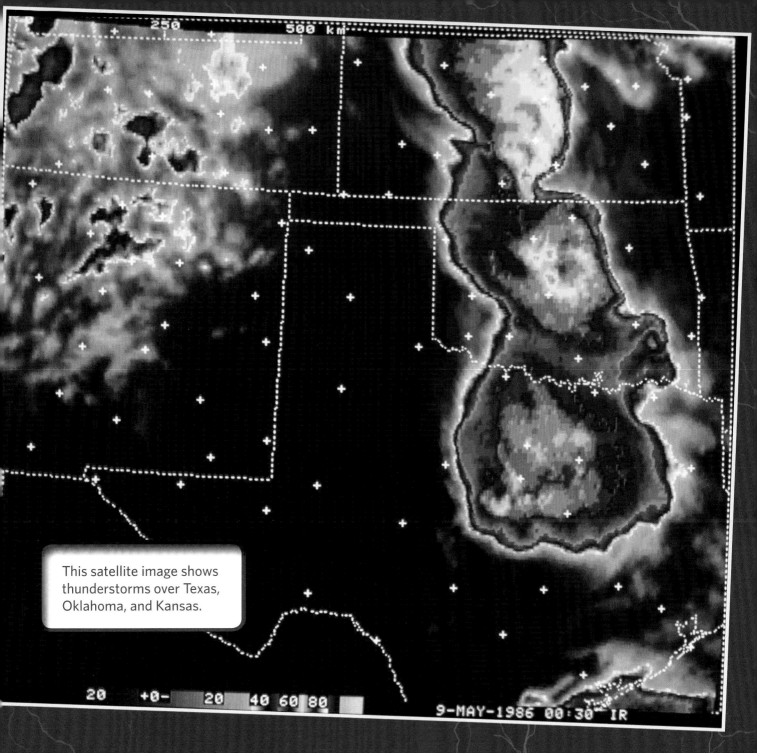

This satellite image shows thunderstorms over Texas, Oklahoma, and Kansas.

250   500 km

20   +0–   20   40 60 80   9-MAY-1986 00:30 IR

Some people go right into storms to learn about them. They are called storm chasers. Storm chasers drive trucks carrying special tools to measure storm winds, temperatures, and moisture.

Scientists use all of this information to build **computer models** of thunderstorms. These help them understand how the next storm might act.

SAFETY FIRST

When the skies turn dark, go inside. Find a local weather report. If a thunderstorm is forming, stay inside until it passes.

If you are caught outside during a storm, stay out of low, narrow areas that might flood. If there is thunder or lightning, get away from tall objects, water, and things made of metal. Crouch down into a tight ball. Being smart during a thunderstorm will keep you safe.

You should stay away from water in a thunderstorm because water conducts, or carries, electricity well.

GLOSSARY

COMPUTER MODELS (kum-PYOO-ter MAH-dulz) Computer programs that show what might happen in real life.

CUMULONIMBUS CLOUDS (kyoo-myuh-luh-NIM-bus KLOWDS) Tall, puffy clouds that bring bad weather.

CUMULUS CLOUDS (KYOO-myuh-lus KLOWDS) Fluffy clouds with flat bottoms.

DOWNDRAFTS (DOWN-drafts) Currents of air that blow downward.

ELECTRIC CHARGE (ih-LEK-trik CHAHRJ) Power that can produce light, heat, or movement.

HAIL (HAYL) Small pieces of ice that fall from the clouds.

LIGHTNING (LYT-ning) A flash of electricity seen as light in the sky.

PARTICLES (PAR-tih-kulz) Small pieces of matter.

RADAR (RAY-dahr) A machine that uses sound waves or radio waves to find objects.

SATELLITES (SA-tih-lyts) Machines in space that circle Earth and that are used to track weather.

TORNADOES (tawr-NAY-dohz) Storms with funnel-shaped clouds that produce strong, spinning winds.

UPDRAFT (UP-draft) A current of air that blows upward.

VAPOR (VAY-per) A liquid that has turned into a gas.

INDEX

WEBSITES

Due to the changing nature of Internet links, PowerKids Press has developed an online list of websites related to the subject of this book. This site is updated regularly. Please use this link to access the list: www.powerkidslinks.com/kd/thund/